PENGUIN BOOKS

Selected Poems: Sophie Hannah

Sophie Hannah was born in Manchester in 1971, and now lives in Bingley, West Yorkshire. She has published four collections of poetry, and is a regular performer of her own work both nationwide and abroad. In 1995 she won an Eric Gregory Award for her first poetry book, *The Hero and the Girl Next Door*, and in 1996 she won an Arts Council Award for her second collection, *Hotels Like Houses*. In June 2004, her fourth poetry book, *First of the Last Chances*, was chosen for the Poetry Book Society's 'Next Generation' promotion. From 1997 to 1999, Sophie was Fellow Commoner in Creative Arts at Trinity College, Cambridge, and from 1999 to 2001 she was a fellow of Wolfson College, Oxford.

Sophie also writes fiction, and won first prize in the 2004 Daphne Du Maurier Festival short-story competition. In May 2007, Sort of Books will publish her first collection of short stories, *We All Say What We Want*. Her latest novel, *Little Face* (2006), is published by Hodder & Stoughton.

More information about Sophie can be found on her website: www.sophiehannah.com.

D1103435

Selected Poems

SOPHIE HANNAH

PENGUIN BOOKS

PENGUIN BOOKS

Published by the Penguin Group
Penguin Books Ltd, 80 Strand, London WC2R ORL, England
Penguin Group (USA) Inc., 375 Hudson Street, New York, New York 10014, USA
Penguin Group (Canada), 90 Eglinton Avenue East, Suite 700, Toronto, Ontario, Canada M4P 2Y3
(a division of Pearson Penguin Canada Inc.)
Penguin Ireland, 25 St Stephen's Green, Dublin 2, Ireland (a division of Penguin Books Ltd)
Penguin Group (Australia), 250 Camberwell Road, Camberwell,
Victoria 3124, Australia (a division of Pearson Australia Group Pty Ltd)
Penguin Books India Pvt Ltd, 11 Community Centre,
Panchsheel Park, New Delhi – 110 017, India
Penguin Group (NZ), cnr Airborne and Rosedale Roads, Albany,
Auckland 1310, New Zealand (a division of Pearson New Zealand Ltd)
Penguin Books (South Africa) (Pty) Ltd, 24 Sturdee Avenue,
Rosebank, Johannesburg 2196, South Africa

Penguin Books Ltd, Registered Offices: 80 Strand, London WC2R ORL, England

www.penguin.com

Some of these poems were first published in *The Hero and the Girl Next Door*,
Hotels Like Houses, *Leaving and Leaving You* and *First of the Last Chances*
(Carcanet Press 1995, 1996, 1999 and 2003 respectively)
This selection first published in Penguin Books 2006
1

Set in Monotype Sabon
Typeset by Rowland Phototypesetting Ltd, Bury St Edmunds, Suffolk
Printed in England by Clays Ltd, St Ives plc

ISBN-13: 978-0-141-02607-7
ISBN-10: 0-141-02607-3

Contents

From *Leaving and Leaving You* (1999)

From *First of the Last Chances* (2003)

New Poems

'No Ball Games etc'

sign outside a London block of flats

Honestly, do we have to spell it out?
No tents, space-hoppers, orgies, Brussels sprout
enthusiasts, no sponsored squirrel fights,
no Ayurvedic quacks, no woolly tights,

no weeping for the joy you think you're owed,
no winking at the house across the road,
dividing rainbows into seven strands
of single colour, no quick show of hands,

no pastry-cutting, origami, chess,
no taking pleasure in your own success,
no sand, no shark impressions, no culottes,
no Christmas pantomimes, no liver spots,

no lurking in the shadows by the shed,
no improvised salutes, no olive bread,
no weightless floating with an auctioneer
in the small pond. No ponds. Hope that's now clear.

Don't Say I Said

Next time you speak to you-know-who
I've got a message for him.
Tell him that I have lost a stone
Since the last time I saw him.
Tell him that I've got three new books
Coming out soon, but play it
Cool, make it sound spontaneous.
Don't say I said to say it.

He might ask if I've mentioned him.
Say I have once, in passing.
Memorize everything he says
And, no, it won't be grassing
When you repeat his words to me –
It's the only way to play it.
Tell him I'm toned and tanned and fine.
Don't say I said to say it.

Say that serenity and grace
Have taken root inside me.
My top-note is frivolity
But beneath, dark passions guide me.
Tell him I'm radiant and replete
And add that every day it

Seems I am harder to resist.
Don't say I said to say it.

Tell him that all my ancient faults
Have been eradicated.
I do not carp or analyse
As I might have when we dated.
Say I'm not bossy any more
Or, better still, convey it
Subtly, but get the point across.
Don't say I said to say it.

Let's Put the Past in Front of Us

Finally we agree. We share a vision.
Allow me to set out in black and white
Our firm, unspoken policy decision.
Feel free to change the parts that don't sound right.

Let's never meet or talk or make things better.
Let's not consider how we each are flawed.
Let's slam down phones and tear up every letter,
And build a silence that could bend a sword.

Let's trample on our friendship, our potential.
Let's blame each other, bitterly, for years.
Let's call our good times false, inconsequential
And frame in gold the doubts, the threats, the tears.

Let's shred our morals, lock away our manners.
Let's cut our feelings off to spite our hearts.
Let's host a carnival of hate, wave banners,
Parade our grudges through the streets, on carts.

Let's not, while we are younger, braver, stronger
Than we will be again, fight hard to save
Lost hope. Whichever one of us lives longer
Can wail 'Too late' beside the other's grave.

If this is not our dream, our aspiration,
Plan A, hooray, what we would both prefer,
Then, in the name of grief and isolation,
Let us at least behave as if it were.

Anyone Can Draw a Line

The day that I got over you
The sun was gold, the sky was blue.
I changed at Sheffield, went by train.
What fate, or sense, had tried in vain
To say so many times before
I heard at last. At last I saw.

What sense, or fate, had tried to say
Was that a stunning summer's day
And all life's other little treats –
Kir Royales, sports cars (leather seats) –
Could never be enhanced by you.
You are not good. You are not true.

You are not brave. You are not sound.
Outside the pub, I looked around.
Your absence gave the village scene
That perfect glow. It might have been
Paradise, or the South of France.
For giving you a second chance

Fate could have scolded me with sleet,
Dark grumbling skies. Instead, a treat

Your joyless hand could not describe.
No chance. This shining day's a bribe
I'm way past ready to accept.
Briefly I missed your rude, inept,

Changeable, narcissistic form.
Then I cheered up. It was so warm,
The sun so bright, the sky so clear
The day I made you disappear:
Today, the twenty-eighth of June.
Have a nice life and afternoon.

Rubbish at Adultery

Must I give up another night
To hear you whinge and whine
About how terribly grim you feel
And what a dreadful swine
You are? You say you'll never leave
Your wife and children. Fine;

When have I ever asked you to?
I'd settle for a kiss.
Couldn't you, for an hour or so,
Just leave them out of *this*?
A rare ten minutes off from guilty
Diatribes – what bliss.

Yes, I'm aware you're sensitive:
A tortured, wounded soul.
I'm after passion, thrills and fun.
You say fun takes its toll,
So what are we doing here? I fear
We've lost our common goal.

You're rubbish at adultery.
I think you ought to quit.
Trouble is, at fidelity
You're also slightly shit.
Choose one and do it properly,
You stupid, stupid git.

From *The Hero and the Girl Next Door* (1995)

One-track Mind

Why does she take unnecessary trips?
She lives just opposite a row of shops.
She went to Crewe to buy a bag of chips.
She went to Birmingham to buy lamb chops.

She has no time for aeroplanes or boats.
She cannot get enough of British Rail.
She went to Liverpool for Quaker Oats
Then Halifax to buy the *Daily Mail*.

She went to Chester for a pair of tights.
Every weekend she's up and down some track.
She went to York for twenty Marlboro Lights.
She went to Stalybridge and came straight back.

Once, on her way to Hull for cottage cheese,
She saw him. All he said was *Tickets, please*.

Before Sherratt & Hughes Became Waterstone's

Romantic entanglements often occur
In a pub or a railway station,
But being a writer I tend to prefer
A suitably bookish location.

I've never liked nightclubs, nor am I the sort
To go for a snog in the loos.
By far the most interesting place to cavort
Is the ground floor of Sherratt & Hughes.

I've seen a few customers looking dismayed,
Too British to voice their objection,
But how can I help it? I like to get laid
Just in front of the poetry section.

Most people prefer a luxurious setting –
A Mediterranean cruise,
But to my mind, the place most conducive to petting
Is the ground floor of Sherratt & Hughes.

All it takes is one glimpse of a gold-lettered spine
On those lovingly organized shelves
And a human encounter seems almost divine –
Not just sex, but a merging of selves.

I have never been someone who strictly adheres
To what's proper – I do as I choose.
(I go down very well with the male cashiers
On the ground floor of Sherratt & Hughes.)

Superstitions

I refuse to share my superstitions with anyone.
You can keep shoes off the table, walk around ladders,
Throw spilt salt over your shoulder, salute single
    magpies –
My behaviour, although insane, is at least original.

I look out of windows but never look into them.
I guard against colds with a fake Scandinavian accent
And I know I will have good luck when my path is
    crossed
Not by a black cat, but by a Chinese man called
    Norman.

This has happened twice in my life (same Norman both
    times).
Long fingernails are a bad omen. When I last grew mine
I found some unexplained underwear in my laundry bag
And was followed home by a man with a bushy
    moustache.

I'm telling the truth. I would never lie on a Friday.
This is not a superstition but what I was taught
By my mother, who used to say if you lose your cat
Give a hedgehog a saucer of milk and hope for the best.

The End of Love

The end of love should be a big event.
It should involve the hiring of a hall.
Why the hell not? It happens to us all.
Why should it pass without acknowledgement?

Suits should be dry-cleaned, invitations sent.
Whatever form it takes – a tiff, a brawl –
The end of love should be a big event.
It should involve the hiring of a hall.

Better than the unquestioning descent
Into the trap of silence, than the crawl
From visible to hidden, door to wall.

Get the announcements made, the money spent.
The end of love should be a big event.
It should involve the hiring of a hall.

Differences

Not everyone who wears a hat
Is copying the Queen.
Not everything that's large and flat
Thinks it's a movie screen.
If every time I dress in blue
I imitate the sea,
It makes no difference what I do –
Nothing is down to me.

Not every dim, electric light
Would like to be the sun.
A water pistol doesn't quite
Mimic a loaded gun.
I do my best, I do my worst
With my specific heart –
God and the Devil got there first;
They had an early start.

Tomatoes can be round and red
Yet be distinct from Mars.
Not all the things above my head
Can be described as stars.

The world had better learn what's what
(If it remotely cares) –
A ladder is a ladder, not
A failed attempt at stairs.

Second Helping of Your Heart

I

I can't remember saying that I wanted this,
But these things happen. (Enter other platitudes.)
I was your midnight scrap. You left your haunted kiss
On my cold lips, without once changing attitudes.

A woman packs a suitcase in the south.
Calf-muscles ache. She may be feeling old tonight,
Or be in bed. Her understudy's mouth
Treats dirty fag-ends like small bars of gold tonight.

I can't remember mixing the ingredients.
Did I or did I not play any part in this?
(Enter a childhood training in obedience.)
Is there a second helping of your heart in this?

The inefficiency of most removal men
Is something that you cannot bear to think about.
Why I should bother chasing your approval when
I disapprove is something I must drink about.

Here, under chilly light and wooden beams,
My thumbnail is too long. It's like a talon.

Here is your parting gift: disruptive dreams
From four till seven. (Enter Woody Allen.)

2

If we examine ratios of power, praise
Becomes a farce. I start to doubt its origin
And its sincerity. Your leaning tower ways
Make bowls of women, fit for slopping porridge in.

Do I have any choice but to give way to you,
Here, in this echo-box? The shadows creep outside.
The sober cynic in me wants to say to you,
'Why bother with me, dear, when there are sheep
    outside?'

But you're too genuine, too off-the-cuff to be
Kept at a distance, treated with disparagement.
Let us not mention what you're old enough to be
Or that you're still not quite sure what your marriage
    meant.

So. Do you really think my work is saleable?
And will your confidence in me deflate a bit
If I declare my body unavailable,
All heavy, disbelieving five foot eight of it?

(Enter a fear of alcohol-dependency,
Tomorrow morning, what the hell I'll say to you.)
I can't risk heights and depths. I have a tendency
To step around such things. And so good day to you.

Wrong Again

I did the right thing once (may God reward me);
Restrained myself. I took a moral stance.
Virtue, I found, was not my thing – it bored me
Rigid, and I would like another chance
To earn myself a wicked reputation
Equal to yours. I'll match you sin for sin.
Lies, promiscuity, inebriation –
It all sounds lovely. When can we begin?
I used to be afraid of rumours spreading.
You made my fear seem fussy, immature.
Here's my new motto, then: just change the bedding
And carry on exactly as before.
A single, happy night beneath your quilt
Is all I want. I'll risk post-coital guilt.

Ghazal

Imagine that a man who never writes
Walks on the planet Mars in cricket whites

Looking for signs of life which isn't there.
He walks through hot red days and dark red nights

Across a surface which is rough and bare.
He feels confused; he's come to see the sights

But there are none, and nobody to share
His empty mouth, his sudden fear of heights.

Nine of his cigarettes are going spare.
The tenth is for himself, and that he lights.

Something's familiar now. He starts to swear.
He stumbles through bizarre, one-sided fights.

Meanwhile you're stuck on Earth without the fare.
In any case, there are no scheduled flights,

And all the love you send is lost in air,
And all your words stick in the sky like kites.

Categories

Some things resist division into parts:
The ventricles and atria of hearts –
The one is at a loss without the other.
The dead son slowly kills the living mother.

The dumbest mouths are those that miss their tongues.
The coldest air is far away from lungs.
Freedom is not what separation brings.
One person takes the bird and one the wings.

Each of us joins a different category
And what is in between ought not to be.

Skipping Rhyme for Graduates

I've got the motive.
I've got the stamina.
I'm going to kill
The external examiner.

Let crows and vultures
Pick at the carcass
After I've murdered
The stingiest of markers.

Bring out the bin-bags.
Bring out the spades.
Bring down the evil sod
Who brings down the grades.

Give me an alibi.
Give me a gun.
Wanted a first
But I got a two-one.

Just missed a first
By a fragment of a fraction.
Justice is called for,
Justice and action.

What a bloody miser!
What a bloody crook!
Won't mark another paper.
Won't write another book.

Won't see his bloody name
In another bloody journal.
Bye-bye, examiner.
Bye-bye, external.

The Hero and the Girl Next Door

This story has at least one side.
The source is quite reliable.
The hero did his best. He tried,
But it was not a viable
Prospect, and so he burned his boats,
He cut his losses, changed his mind,
Dry-cleaned his most attractive coats
And left the girl next door behind.

His Christmas list had shed a name.
The girl next door had shed some tears,
But she was utterly to blame,
Had been, in fact, for several years.
Rewind. The lady vanishes.
Press stop, fast forward, then eject.
And what a silly girl she is.
And does she honestly expect . . .

So this is provocation, then,
And this is what they call just cause
And this is how you see it when
The hero is a friend of yours.

Another soldier saves his skin.
Another wrinkle ironed out.
You bet. You roll the dice. You win.
There is no reasonable doubt.

A Day Too Late

You meet a man. You're looking for a hero,
Which you pretend he is. A day too late
You realize his sex appeal is zero
And you begin to dread the second date.

You'd love to stand him up but he's too clever –
He knows by heart your work and home address.
Last night he said he'd stay with you forever.
You fear he might have meant it. What a mess!

That's when you start regretting his existence.
It's all his fault. You hate him with a passion.
You hate his love, his kindness, his persistence.
He's too intense. His clothes are out of fashion.

Shortly you reach the stage of desperation.
At first you thought about behaving well
And giving him an honest explanation.
Now all you want to say is 'Go to Hell',

And even that seems just a touch too gentle.
Deep down, the thing that makes you want to weep
Is knowing that you once felt sentimental
About this wholly unattractive creep.

Trainers All Turn Grey

(after Robert Frost's 'Nothing Gold Can Stay')

You buy your trainers new.
They cost a bob or two.
At first they're clean and white,
The laces thick and tight.
Then they must touch the ground –
(You have to walk around).
You learn to your dismay
Trainers all turn grey.

The Fairy Never Came to Get My Teeth

How can I help? I don't know when to clap
And when to throw a fit. It's not my day.
I've got a notebook sitting on my lap.
I can't get up until it goes away.

How do the neighbours know your bones are brittle?
I hear it from above you and beneath.
How's this for relevance: when I was little
The fairy never came to get my teeth.

I'm one of them, no longer one of us.
I haven't got the knack of self-expression
Like others have. I never make a fuss
Or jump the queue. I'm in the wrong profession.

The sawn-off shotgun in your biscuit tin,
The headless rodent in your Christmas stocking,
May drive me mad, but I will not barge in.
We're quaint round here. We still believe in knocking.

The smartest pupil in the haystack class
Pontificates all night: attack, defend . . .
Meanwhile there's no one sweeping up the glass.
What you need most is not another friend,

Another eager face behind the door
To make you circulate a false address.
I keep away. Ask yourself who cares more.
A bigger crowd creates a bigger mess.

What do I think about an early grave?
Head-on collision with a wall or tree?
I think it's neither glamorous nor brave.
You need a louder audience than me.

You need a quiet night without a row.
You need a holiday. You need a fling.
(I hear my mother say *Be careful now*
And my reply: *I am becarefulling.*)

Leaving the house, dizzy from lack of lunch,
I pass two cold burritos in a trilby.
Each flippant story packs a careful punch.
It's not your day. I doubt it ever will be.

Mountains Out of Small Hills

Dogs are objecting to the word dogmatic,
the use of certain phrases – barking mad,
dog in the manger. Equally emphatic
are other species. Rats and snakes have had

enough of being symbols of deceit
and treachery. They say there's no excuse,
and there are fish protesting on the street
at being linked with alcohol abuse.

You couldn't taunt a coward nowadays
with 'scaredy-cat' or 'chicken'. Cock-and-bull
stories have been renamed. Nobody says
'God, she's a cow!' Nobody pulls the wool

over another person's eyes – the lambs
have seen to that. Nobody rabbits on.
Nor has there been a ramraid since the rams
petitioned parliament. We do not swan

around, get goosebumps; nothing gets our goat.
No cricket player ever scores a duck.
Once we were free with what we said and wrote.
Now we make do with swear-words. Bollocks. Fuck.

Morning Has Broken

The shark in *Jaws* was a lovable household pet.
Butch Cassidy and Sundance didn't die.
Scarlett and Rhett
did not split up. They gave it another try.

And you're a good egg, safe bet,
real brick. You're an honest guy.

The encounter was not so brief.
The bodies were never snatched.
Clyde Barrow wasn't a thief.

You're available, unattached –
no partner to give you grief.
We are well-matched.

Bergman and Bogart got back together
after the end of *Casablanca*.

I'm not at the end of my tether
and you're not a wanker.

As for last night,
neither my feelings nor my drinks were mixed
and it looks the same in the light.
Morning is fixed.

The Affair

The lamp post bends his head. His face is red
above the frozen fringes of the street.
Dishevelled night is climbing into bed.
She strokes the waking clock, then steals the sheet.

Something disturbs the symmetry of hedges;
a recent scandal seeping through the grass.
The breathing curtains lose their heavy edges,
touched by the light that settles on the glass.

A small dog kicks the pavement into stretching.
The postbox mouth hangs open for receiving.
I almost hear a taxi driver fetching
your suitcase. Very soon you will be leaving.

Summary of a Western

We see a dusty desert scene and that's
The way the film begins. Some men in hats
Deliver gritty lines. They all wear braces.
They're cool and tough. They hate the darker races
Who paint peculiar stripes across their faces.

Goodies meet baddies, mostly in corrals.
Cowboys ignore or patronize their gals.
We see a gun twirl in a macho hand.
Who's killing whom we don't quite understand –
There's always some vague reference to the land.

Women in aprons have to be protected.
Stagecoaches fall. New sheriffs are elected.
The cast consists primarily of horses –
They gallop to the ending, which of course is
A happy one, where nobody divorces.

The Answer

Why do you give the impression that you'd rather
not be loved? You almost tell people not to bother.
Why are you neither one thing nor the other?

Why do you fluctuate between ticks and crosses,
alternate between flippancy and neurosis?
Won't you confirm or contradict my guesses?

What is it that you do, by simply sitting
with your elbows raised, that makes me sick of
      waiting?
Why is your absence tantamount to cheating?

I know you're real, which means you must pay taxes,
catch colds and snore. I know you know what sex is.
Still, there is something in you that never mixes,

something that smells like the air in silver boxes.

It makes me suddenly afraid of asking,
suddenly sure of all the things I'm risking.

A *Fairly Universal Set*

Whoever cleans your windows once a week,
Whoever stuffs your letters through the door,
Whoever you'd get in to fix a leak –
I resent all of these and plenty more.

Men on the bus and women in the street,
Religious nuts who ring your bell at dawn,
Any chiropodist who's touched your feet,
Canvassers, tramps, whoever mows your lawn,

Your colleagues, friends, acquaintances (both sexes),
People with whom you've shared a cigarette,
Your enemies, and, most of all, your exes,
Everyone you have ever seen or met,

Voices you might from time to time have heard,
The speaking clock. Jealous is not the word.

When Will You Come and Identify My Body?

When will you come and identify my body?
It had better be soon or I might just take it amiss.
When will you come and identify my body?
Men basically do what they want, and I've only just
    realized this.

It was silly of me to drown in a shallow river,
Too small a gesture to impress the boys.
It was silly of me to drown in a shallow river.
They are either silent, or else they are making their
    football noise.

I would like to be buried with my shampoo and
    conditioner.
Once I was self-obsessed and even clean.
I would like to be buried with my shampoo and
    conditioner.
I'm aware that the cricket highlights start at eleven
    fifteen.

I have been deacidified and boxed.
You shouldn't have left me. You shouldn't have gone
    to the bar.

I have been deacidified and boxed.
You'll find me in pepper and pickle. You'll find me
    under the car

Or creeping up behind you with a trowel.
Are you a garlic crusher or a torch?
I'm creeping up behind you with a trowel.
You would never change. You would never redecorate
    the porch.

It's clear to me from the way you keep escaping
(Into halls, through doors) that you will never be ready.
It's clear, from me to the way you keep escaping.
When, though? When will you come? Will you come
    and identify my body?

Triskaidekaphobia

Is it as easy as you make it sound?
You tell me not to cry on your account.
You didn't cry. I doubt you even frowned.
You sleep too easily when I'm around.
If I'm too much, are you the right amount?

This is about as open as I get.
Gram Parsons said love hurts and I agree
Although I haven't said I love you yet
And therefore have no right to be upset
Because you don't say anything to me.

We've really taken safety to extremes.
Reluctance makes us both insensitive.
They may come true, but would we call them dreams?
We're playground captains, calmly picking teams,
And even if there's nothing to forgive

You're hardly what a nice young girl expects,
If I can still describe myself as such –
Prostitutes, dogs and strange religious sects,
Your special drug and alcohol effects.
The message on your back reads please don't touch.

I see a threat in every paragraph,
Subject each letter to analysis.
I try and fail (you just can't get the staff)
To resurrect the flirt that made you laugh
But find her taking all your jokes amiss,

And all your views on dolls and boxing rings.
It's good to see your well-proportioned mind
Is on top form and full of different things.
Were you a child who didn't fall off swings
Unless there was a mattress close behind?

All right, I'm being totally unfair
But silence always makes me want to rant,
Like sneaking through the nothing to declare
Gate at the airport. I can hardly bear
Your morning walks. You're far too much like Kant.

A bit more truth over a few more days
And maybe panic would give way to sense.
Look at me now. I take a simple phrase
And blow it up in twelve pedantic ways,
Not out of spite, merely as self-defence.

This dot to dot is less than we deserve,
One of the many things I wish I'd said.
Until such time as I can find the nerve
I'll walk in ways that make the traffic swerve
And try to stop you getting out of bed.

An Aerial View

Flight 608. The woman to my right
Has hardly touched the meal Air France provided.
She prods it with her fork as though she might,
Probably won't, but hasn't quite decided.

She eyes my empty tray with vague distaste –
I ate it all, and we were given loads.
She's proud of her restraint, her slender waist.
Neither will help her if the plane explodes.

She's frowning at my bottle of champagne,
Perhaps because it's only 8 a.m.,
But I don't care. When I am on a plane
My motto is 'enjoy myself – stuff them'.

Long-face can stick to water all the way,
That's up to her. I don't intend to slum it.
I'm pissed. She never drinks before midday.
Irrelevant distinction, if we plummet.

Last chance, perhaps, for grub and heavy drinking.
One shouldn't miss it. Here's what I advise:
Light up a fag, and concentrate on thinking
An aeroplane is just a pub that flies.

From *Hotels Like Houses* (1996)

Lusting After Walter Knife

They mention him without intent
And you pretend you haven't heard
Anything more than what was meant
Because his name's a household word.

Imagine – loving Peter Chair
Would make deciding where to sit
Almost impossible to bear
If you connected him with it,

Or lusting after Walter Knife –
One move to spread your margarine
Might make you want to stab his wife;
Not what things are but what they mean

To you, so dig a hole and hide
Unless his name is Pete or Loam
And if the man's called Mountainside
You might be better off at home.

Preventative Elegy

There will not be a burial,
There will not be a wake.
No ashes will be sprinkled
Over the stream or lake.
There won't be a cremation,
A coffin or a shroud.
No hearse will park along the road –
Your death is not allowed.

There will not be a graveyard,
There'll be no marble stone
Bearing a carved endearment.
No flesh will shrink to bone
And in the town that loves you
There'll be no sobbing crowd.
No one inherits anything –
Your death is not allowed.

No grief will need to be disguised
As just a bit upset.
No one will wonder whether to
Remember or forget
Or which would cause the greater pain,
And whether we laughed or rowed

Last time will be irrelevant –
Your death is not allowed.

Others will die instead of you.
A fixed amount must die
(If there are quotas with these things)
And strangers' wives will cry
But I will have no need to say
I loved you and was proud
To be what I have been to you –
Your death is not allowed.

Person Specification

The ideal candidate for the position
of soulmate to the all-important you
should say she loves you, of her own volition,
every five minutes, and it should be true.

She must be motivated and ambitious
but feminine. She will be good at art,
at homely things. Her meals should be nutritious.
The ideal candidate will win your heart

with her prowess in bed. She will look stunning
in public, turn at least ten heads per day.
She should do most of (if not all) the running
and be prepared for marriage straight away.

Points will be lost for boring occupations,
excessive mood swings, drugs and other men.
To those who fail, your deep commiserations.
This post will not be advertised again.

Darling Sweatheart

He couldn't spell. The letters were addressed
to *Darling Sweatheart*, though he acted mean
when I was with him. Probably the best
present he gave me was some margarine –

a tub of Stork, half full. It wasn't wrapped.
He shrugged and said *You might as well have this.*
He'd find excuses, say his lips were chapped
in an attempt to dodge my weekly kiss.

He'd made a comprehensive wedding plan
involving just the two of us. No way
were guests allowed. His dog would be Best Man.
I dithered. *What a life* he used to say,

Let's have a kid. If we get skint, we'll sell it.
He wasn't bad. It's just the way I tell it.

To Whom It May Concern at the Whalley Range Driving Test Centre

Please don't regard this as a threat.
We'll be the best of friends, I bet,
Though up to now we've never met
And I'd just like the chance to get
Some feelings off my chest,

Which won't take very long to read.
The point is this: I must succeed.
I'll never drink and drive or speed.
I really want and really need
To pass my driving test,

And, well, if God forbid I fail
I'll stand outside your house and wail,
Circle your place of work and trail
Black L-plates from a black gauze veil.
I'll be the petrol guest

At every gathering you host,
Proposing a malignant toast,
A sickly, seatbelt-wearing ghost,
Liking you least instead of most.
I'll never let you rest

And may your Fiat Tipo burn.
Sorry. That sounds a little stern.
My nerves are bad. Tonight I learn
Left hand reverse and three point turn
So wish me all the best.

Neither Home Nor Dry

No need to put your magazine away
If there's an article you want to read;
I could just sit and look at you all day.
Were you about to speak to me? No need.
My minimum is very bare indeed.

I'm happy eating breakfast on my own
Knowing that you are in a room nearby,
Smugly asleep. I'm happy to postpone
Thought and decision, question and reply
For now, since I am neither home nor dry.

You want to stir your drink? I'll fetch a spoon.
I'll wear my heels down looking at the sights
Because you say I should. We're leaving soon.
I watch the pattern form. I may have rights
But no time has been set aside for fights.

Soon I'll be in my favourite service station
(Well-named, because it is a welcome break),
Eating a slice of sickly *Fudge Temptation*
As usual. With such a lot at stake
It's comforting to recognize a cake.

Hotels Like Houses

She is the one who takes a shine
to ceilings and to floors,
whose eye finds room for every line
scratched on the wardrobe doors.

She thinks in terms of thick red rope
around the bed, a plaque
above the hardened bathroom soap.
He's always first to pack.

If their affair has awkward spells,
what's bound to cause the rows is
that he treats houses like hotels
and she, hotels like houses.

When He's at Home

A patch provokes the lazy eye,
Pillars support the dome.
I say his name and friends reply
Who's he when he's at home?

He's a performing art on stage.
At work he's smart and busy.
He's Times New Roman on the page.
When he's at home, who is he?

He's the road atlas man in cars.
On fairground rides he's dizzy.
He's wet in rain and drunk in bars.
When he's at home, who is he,

When there is nothing that provokes
And when there's no support?
Nothing. The show is over, folks,
And sooner than I thought.

Loss Adjuster

Scale down your expectations once again
from rest of life to years to one whole night
to will he wander past a phone or pen.
If he would only either ring or write.
Get real and scale those expectations down
from conversation to a single word –
seen through the window of a shop in town
if not by you then by a trusted third
party, or, if a sighting is too much
to hope for (as undoubtedly it is)
scale down your hopes and aim to see or touch
someone whose name sounds similar to his.
A scale of one to ten. Two weeks ago
he dared to keep you waiting while he slept.
Scale down much further and today's poor show
tomorrow you'll be happy to accept.

Fair to Say

It's fair to say you own a boat. It's yours.
Nothing luxurious. A rowing boat.
First it springs holes and then you lose the oars.
It's when the thing can barely stay afloat
Let alone speed you off to foreign shores –
At that point you no longer have a boat.

You rent a flat, a corrugated box,
No fancy furnishings, no welcome mat.
One day the landlord changes all the locks.
A dog moves in. It tries to kill your cat.
It's when the door stays closed, despite your knocks –
At that point you no longer have a flat.

You've got a boss. You've worked for him for years.
He is a firm, authoritative boss
Until one day the office disappears.
You ask him what to do. He's at a loss.
He looks away and covers up his ears –
At that point you no longer have a boss.

As for your man, the things he used to do
Like smile and speak, watch movies, make a plan,

Listen to music, kiss – to name a few –
He's given up, as if some kind of ban
Were on them all. When somebody who blew
Hot now blows cold and you've done all you can –
At that point you no longer have a man.

When his turned back makes one bed feel like two –
At that point you no longer have a clue.

The During Months

Like summer in some countries and like rain
in mine, for nuns like God, for drunks like beer,
like food for chefs, for invalids like pain,
you've occupied a large part of the year.

The during months to those before and since
would make a ratio of ten to two,
counting the ones spent trying to convince
myself there was a beating heart in you

when diagrams were all you'd let me see.
Hearts should be made of either blood or stone,
or both, like mine. There's still December free –
the month in which I'll save this year, alone.

The Mind I Lose

Whether the things I feel are true
or just illusion on my part,
I think that I'm in love with you
and wouldn't want to doubt my heart.

You say my heart may not exist.
I know it does, but isn't what
I once believed. This adds a twist,
the like of which can save a plot.

Feelings and thoughts are kept apart
unfairly by the words we choose.
Find me a better name than heart
by which to call the mind I lose.

The Sight of Mares

Either a dark horse, not a horse at all,
or else a horse resentful of the label,
at giddy-ups he turns to face the wall.
He says he's never been inside a stable.

I take his word for it (he ought to know),
but others disagree and say he moves
just like a horse. Explain, then, why he's so
uncomfortable with the idea of hooves

and why he shudders at the sight of mares
and all the other things you can't explain.
Four legs he may have – so do beds and chairs,
but something makes you call his hair a mane

and you imagine he must have a tail
though you would never say so to his face,
not when he puts his saddle up for sale
and says he hasn't heard about the race

in which all horses should be taking part.
He seems sincere, but bear in mind, of course,
even if he is not a horse at heart
that doesn't mean he's not, in fact, a horse,

though given all the medals he could win
being a horse, it's odd that he would choose
not to be one. You ought to see him grin
when he pulls off his semi-circle shoes.

Ms Quicksand is a Bitch

Reflected personality –
defence and favoured myth
of Mrs Smith, whose treachery
is loved by Mr Smith.

Husband is nice so wife must be
when right beside the moans
of Mrs Jones, what do you see?
The smile of Mr Jones.

Mrs Brown's shoes have heavy soles
for treading people down
while badgers, dolphins, bears and moles
are saved by Mr Brown.

When Mrs House (née Flat) agreed
to marry Mr House
she must have known that she would need
a mitigating spouse

but would he live with, sleep with, stay
with, would he share a bed . . . ?
Yes, and you see it every day,
the wed, the not yet wed –

If mountaintops were not too high
to recognize a ditch,
then Mr Hill would not deny
Ms Quicksand is a bitch.

She Can Win Favour

Her friend the locksmith readily believes
the tales she tells of all the locks she's picked.
She can win favour with a gang of thieves
by itemizing all the goods she's nicked,
and then you hear her talking to a judge
about the many crimes she has prevented.
Confectioners are told she's fond of fudge,
landlords, about the properties she's rented.
She can be just like anyone she meets
by flicking through her catalogue of poses –
ally of underdogs and of élites,
to gardeners she boasts of pruning roses,
to firemen of the time she braved the fire –
never to liars, though, that she's a liar.

On the Silver Side

However you may be under a different bridge,
under this one you're luminous and round,
watch-faced or moon-faced, split, on the silver side,
glowing right through me as I begin sprouting wires.

I have looked for you under the bridge of the curling
    stones,
under the oily bridge and under the fence
that believes it's a bridge. You aren't under any of
    those,
however you may be under a different bridge,

one made of shells and crowns and packs of cards,
coliseums and changing rooms, but you'd better not be
under my bridge wishing you were somewhere else.
However you may be under a different bridge.

Glass Eyebrow

the end   an eyebrow   where I draw the line
glass eyebrow   I occasionally raise
for company   only the Shugborough sign
only an eyebrow misses you   bouquets

The Shugborough sign has seen me go South East,
has seen me head South West and to the coast.
The Shugborough sign has seen me as the least
important person, seen me as the most,
and on some trips I turn to it and boast.

the end an eyebrow where I draw the line

Some people never see the Shugborough sign.
They pass it half asleep or in a daze.
No one has claimed it so it must be mine
glass eyebrow I occasionally raise
glass eyebrows on selected motorways.

Drivers have hurtled past the white and brown
Shugborough sign and passengers have dozed,
while I have passed the A-road to your town,
many a time, pretending it was closed

or not a possibility   my head
that it went wrong   for which I do not blame
the motorways   for even though they led
to you   may lead to better things   the same

Negotiate the fairest deal you can
although it might mean pulling punks from trees.
Those of us searching for a Shugborough man
request a motorway extension, please.

So bless so bless the Shugborough sign and praise
even the signs you may not understand.
You see them by the sides of motorways
but can't imagine what they might have planned:

a parrot as a substitute for words,
a festival assistant with a sneer
fluttering slowly to a world of birds.
The Shugborough man has missed another year,

but he is coming just as you were not,
and meanwhile life goes on and plastic trays
bring all-day brunches and the weather's hot

only an eyebrow misses you   bouquets

Ticket to Staines

I'd emerged from the second of two freezing trains
With a bag full of cheese salad sandwich remains
When I met a tree surgeon who said he was broke
And asked me to buy him a ticket to Staines.

He told me a jumbled, unfortunate tale
About how he had broken the terms of his bail
And he had to get back to his mum's before ten
Or the cops would be taking him straight back to jail.

He told me his story outside Euston station
Describing his crime and its justification:
His tree surgeon's chainsaw had sliced through a train
In an effort to sabotage veal transportation.

His mum had lumbago and no credit card
For a telephone booking. I thought long and hard
And it seemed to be me and me only that stood
Between him and a grilling at New Scotland Yard.

With diminishing faith in the state of my brains
And without quite condoning the slicing of trains
I led him past Knickerbox, Sock Shop and all
And bought that tree surgeon a ticket to Staines.

What will become of him? Where will he go?
(And don't say, 'You paid for it, you ought to know.')
I mean, is there a place for him? Is there a place
For a lawbreaking tree surgeon, chainsaw in tow?

There's a place for the tyrant who rules and constrains,
For the person who keeps other people in chains.
Wherever that tree surgeon goes, freedom reigns.
I wish I could see him arriving in Staines.

Soft-handed Man

She couldn't love a man who had soft hands
and didn't do constructive things with wood,
but if she met one that she loved, she could.
She's right to say we all make strange demands
and right to think that no one understands.
Hard hands are not indicative of good

character, don't infallibly belong
to rugged, silent types who rarely shave,
who are, in equal measures, kind and brave.
Just over the horizon there's a strong
soft-handed man waiting to prove her wrong,
and when a person proves you wrong, they save

acres of mind you were about to close
and turn it into habitable land.
Each time you hold an unexpected hand
and stare at features that you never chose,
you're dealing with authority that knows
better than you how well things can be planned.

Postcard from a Travel Snob

I do not wish that anyone were here.
This place is not a holiday resort
with karaoke nights and pints of beer
for drunken tourist types – perish the thought.

This is a peaceful place, untouched by man –
not like your seaside-town-consumer-hell.
I'm sleeping in a local farmer's van –
it's great. There's not a guest house or hotel

within a hundred miles. Nobody speaks
English (apart from me, and rest assured,
I'm not your sun-and-sangria-two-weeks-
small-minded-package-philistine-abroad).

When you're as multi-cultural as me,
your friends become wine connoisseurs, not drunks.
I'm not a British tourist in the sea;
I am an anthropologist in trunks.

My Enemies

My enemies, polished inside their caskets
My enemies sparkle behind glass doors
My enemies, curled into tilted baskets
My enemies, not yours

my enemies   You cannot steal or hire them
my enemies   You cannot loan or share
my enemies   Don't tidy or admire them
Don't even see them there

my enemies   Steer clear of the display case
My enemies try to make false amends
my enemies   The pallor of your grey face
will make them shine like friends

My enemies, proud of their faults and failings
my enemies   You take them out for tea
My enemies, beckoning through the railings
at a novice enemy

My enemies will give you proper training
My enemies shuffle up shelves for you
my enemies   The old ones are complaining
I like them better new

74

my   a new enemy   an equidistant
enemy showing every friend the door
politely, like a personal assistant
my enemies   One more

A Strong Black Coffee for the Sleeping Dog

They let you in. You interrupt their dinner.
You're on your back instead of on your knees.
If you behave yourself, one day you'll win a
Glimpse of your loved one's chips and mushy peas.
     What do I have to do to be a sinner?
     Turn a saint's pencil forty-five degrees.

He had a small square yard for us to smoke in,
Behind a hut and safe from parish spies.
The room his parents used to put strange folk in
Was also square and of a matching size.
     I listened to the same twelve songs and spoke in
     The hushed tones of a consolation prize.

Perhaps I wasn't any consolation.
Perhaps he didn't want to be consoled.
Years ago, when he had an explanation
And would have told me, I would not be told.
     I hang around the graveyard and the station,
     Outside the dog-eared college, feeling old,

And glamorize the benches and the matches.
I put the faces back inside the room.

His jacket with the shiny shoulder patches –
Does he still have it and, if not, to whom
      Does it belong? One drops, another catches.
      One has a spade and plenty to exhume.

By now you will be guessing my agenda,
That I am here for reasons of my own,
Not being shy or wise enough to send a
Token or two then leave you all alone.
      I'm here in what should be my place, to spend a
      Day with a gentleman I should have known.

Since neither of the heartless queens is present,
I have become a princess not a frog
As far as he's concerned, but what bland, pleasant
Creature might he be stalking through the fog?
      I've got a croissant shaped just like a crescent,
      A strong black coffee for the sleeping dog.

I've come to demonstrate that to be able
Is what counts most. Too late and not too late
Have been defined today, and though unstable
Has given way to steady, mad to great,
      If he still keeps those objects on his table,
      There is a sort of chance, at any rate.

Pink and the Gang

Pink house in a grey town,
Thin house on a long street,
White stone house and brown –
All raise their rents to beat

The house that won't compete –
The tall house by the sea
Who says, to cries of cheat,
Do not charge rent for me.

However loud his voice
They'll make their rents as large.
They will be seen as choice;
He, as ashamed to charge.

White, brown, pink and thin
Monopolize the streets.
Materialists move in,
Are rewarded with receipts

While the tall sea house takes
Nothing but love and thanks
From his tenant, who mistakes
Pink and the gang for banks.

The Good Loser

I have portrayed temptation as amusing.
Now he can either waver or abstain.
His is a superior kind of losing
And mine is an inferior brand of gain.

His sacrifice, his self-imposed restriction
Will get through this controversy intact
For his is a superior kind of fiction
And mine is an inferior brand of fact.

I have displayed my most attractive feature
And he his least, yet still the match seems odd.
For I am a superior kind of creature
And he is an inferior brand of god

And if he cuts me off without a warning
His is the book from which I'll take a leaf
For his is a superior kind of mourning
And ours a most inferior brand of grief.

When a Poet Loves a Composer

One look at him and I forgot
Embarrassingly soon
That music ought to have, if not
Lyrics, at least a tune.

He's highbrow in a big, big way
But when he sees that I'm
The one, he'll think that it's okay
For poetry to rhyme.

From *Leaving and Leaving You*
(1999)

Occupational Hazard

He has slept with accountants and brokers,
With a cowgirl (well, someone from Healds).
He has slept with non-smokers and smokers
In commercial and cultural fields.

He has slept with book-keepers, book-binders,
Slept with auditors, florists, PAs,
Child psychologists, even child minders,
With directors of firms and of plays.

He has slept with the stupid and clever.
He has slept with the rich and the poor
But he sadly admits that he's never
Slept with a poet before.

Real poets are rare, he confesses,
While it's easy to find a cashier.
So I give him some poets' addresses
And consider a change of career.

In Wokingham on Boxing Day at The Edinburgh Woollen Mill

Two earnest customers compare
a ribbed and unribbed sleeve.
I wonder what I'm doing here
and think I ought to leave,
get in my car and drive away.
       I stand beside the till
       in Wokingham on Boxing Day
       at The Edinburgh Woollen Mill.

All of the other shops are closed.
Most people are in bed.
Somehow I know that I'm supposed
to find an A–Z.
Somehow I sense I must obey
       an unfamiliar will
       in Wokingham on Boxing Day
       at The Edinburgh Woollen Mill.

I parked in a disabled space
so either I'm a cheat
or a debilitating case
of searching for your street

has started to erode away
        my locomotive skill
        in Wokingham on Boxing Day
        at The Edinburgh Woollen Mill,

somewhere perhaps you've never been.
I doubt you're into wool.
Even if mohair's not your scene
the atmosphere is full
of your proximity. I sway
        and feel a little ill
        in Wokingham on Boxing Day
        at The Edinburgh Woollen Mill.

The sales assistants wish me luck
and say they hope I find
the place I want. I have been stuck
with what I left behind,
with what I've been too scared to say,
        too scared to say until
        in Wokingham on Boxing Day
        at The Edinburgh Woollen Mill

I tell myself the time is now;
willingly I confess
my love for you to some poor cow
in an angora dress

whose *get lost loony* eyes convey
      her interest, which is nil,
      in Wokingham on Boxing Day
      at The Edinburgh Woollen Mill.

I find your house. You're still in bed.
I leave my gift and flee,
pleased with myself, not having said
how you can contact me,
driven by fears I can't allay,
      dreams I did not fulfil
      in Wokingham on Boxing Day
      at The Edinburgh Woollen Mill.

Chains are the most distressing shops.
They crop up everywhere.
The point at which the likeness stops
squeezes my lungs of air.
When I see jumpers on display
      I wish that I was still
      in Wokingham on Boxing Day
      at The Edinburgh Woollen Mill.

Diminishing Returns

I will tell outright lies where you embellish.
Your yawn will be my cue to fall asleep.
Anyone who is watching us with relish
Will find that, where your talk and tricks are cheap,
Mine will be cast-offs. When you stop at kissing
I'll stop at shaking hands; you eye the clock,
I'll grab my watch and gasp at what I'm missing
And any door you close, I'll double-lock.
Operate slowly – I'll stand still for ever.
Leave quickly – I will be the speed of light
Passing you on the way, and if we never
Do anything constructive, that's all right
(Though it will be a wasted chance) because
While casual observers say of you
'He led her on', of me they'll say, 'She was
The less enthusiastic of the two.'

Against Road-building

He hated roads. He loved the land.
He tended to forget
Or else he didn't understand
That roads were how we met.

He loved long walks. He hated cars.
He often put them down.
Without them, though, I'd have reached Mars
Before I reached his town.

Now that I've seen bad air pervade
An atmosphere once sweet
I wish the car was never made
That drove me to his street.

Now that I've felt a world explode
As I had not before
I wish they'd never built the road
That led me to his door.

Your Dad Did What?

Where they have been, if they have been away,
or what they've done at home, if they have not –
you make them write about the holiday.
One writes *My Dad did*. What? Your Dad did what?

That's not a sentence. Never mind the bell.
We stay behind until the work is done.
You count their words (you who can count and spell);
all the assignments are complete bar one

and though this boy seems bright, that one is his.
He says he's finished, doesn't want to add
anything, hands it in just as it is.
No change. *My Dad did*. What? What did his Dad?

You find the 'E' you gave him as you sort
through reams of what this girl did, what that lad did,
and read the line again, just one 'e' short:
This holiday was horrible. My Dad did.

If People Disapprove of You . . .

Make being disapproved of your hobby.
Make being disapproved of your aim.
Devise new ways of scoring points
In the Being Disapproved Of Game.

Let them disapprove in their dozens.
Let them disapprove in their hordes.
You'll find that being disapproved of
Builds character, brings rewards

Just like any form of striving.
Don't be arrogant; don't coast
On your high disapproval rating.
Try to be disapproved of most.

At this point, if it's useful,
Draw a pie chart or a graph.
Show it to someone who disapproves.
When they disapprove, just laugh.

Count the emotions you provoke:
Anger, suspicion, shock.
One point for each of these and two
For every boat you rock.

Feel yourself warming to your task –
You do it bloody well.
At last you've found an area
In which you can excel.

Savour the thrill of risk without
The fear of getting caught.
Whether they sulk or scream or pout,
Enjoy your new-found sport.

Meanwhile, all those who disapprove
While you are having fun
Won't even know your game exists
So tell yourself you've won.

The Wise One

I could not scrub the lift shaft with a toothbrush,
Spare time to stitch new bookmarks out of lace
Or carry boxes up and down rope ladders.
I'm not the helpful one around this place.
The helpful one is over there with a chipped marble
    face.

I will not press a calculator's buttons,
Clock in, tot up, give coins as change from notes.
I'm not the numbers one. Haven't they told you
How dizzy I am from counting last year's votes?
The numbers one is on the slab, under a pile of
    coats.

Don't come to me for vases of carnations –
I'd barely know a cactus from a rose.
Consult the experts for the best arrangements,
Flowery ones. I am not one of those.
The flowery one is in the earth, with everything that
    grows.

I haven't seen the overhead projector
This week. I cannot just nip down the road.
I'm not the knowing one, I'm not the going one,

Or the finding one. Those three are being towed
To a farm to be written out of a crucial episode.

Which one am I? I must be one. Everyone else is.
Look at those little pet other ones, shining their knees,
No doubts as to which ones they are. Which one am I?
The answering one, the resolving one? Neither of these.
Try the wise one, the free one, but only if everyone else
    agrees.

Driving Me Away

I caught the train to Waterloo,
The tube to Leicester Square.
Both did what they set out to do,
But neither could compare
With your closed eyes, your bitten nails
And the oddness you display.
You beat whatever's on the rails
At driving me away.

The coach to Gatwick last July
Did it in record time.
The plane, once it had deigned to fly,
Managed an upward climb.
You beat whatever's in the air
Or on the motorway
And do not even charge a fare
For driving me away.

The transit van I hired to move
For which I had to pack
Box after box, as if to prove
I wasn't coming back
And before driving which I paid
A visit to the tip,

Just to ensure the point was made:
This was a one-way trip –

You beat that too. I could name loads
Of engine-powered things
In oceans, in the clouds, on roads,
With carriages or wings
But you could nudge them all off track
With the mad things you say.
No car could ever have your knack
Of driving me away.

There's not a lot that you can do
Well, or indeed at all.
I must appreciate your few
Talents. When taxis stall
Or when friends offer me a lift
And there's a slight delay
I am reminded of your gift
For driving me away.

None of the Blood

None of the blood that is in your body
   is in my body. None of the blood
      that is in my body is in your body.
Whatever you are, you are not my blood.

None of the flesh that is on your body
   is on my body. None of the flesh
      that is on my body is on your body.
Whatever you are, you are not my flesh.

I have shared a bottle of wine with a bigot
   (none of the eggshells, none of the mud
      in my kitchen and garden, your kitchen and
        garden).
None of the flesh. None of the blood

that is in my kitchen is in your kitchen.
   (I am being rude. I am not just being rude.)
      None of your garden is in my garden.
I have shared a picnic bench with a prude.

Furniture, yes, means of transport, yes,
   but no to soul and no to bone
      (none of your sellotape, none of your glue).
Yes to some stranger. No to you.

Marrying the Ugly Millionaire

Here comes my mother carrying
Dried flowers for my hair.
This afternoon I'm marrying
The ugly millionaire.

Here is my sister with the veil.
Everyone wants to share
My lucrative unholy grail –
The ugly millionaire.

There are our presents, wrapped and tied.
Soon they will fill the room.
All marked (no mention of the bride)
Attention of the groom –

No Dior, no St Laurent, no frills,
No full Le Creuset set.
Only my father's unpaid bills,
My brother's gambling debt,

Demands beyond and way above
What would be right or fair.
I hate the grasping lot. I love
The ugly millionaire.

Next Door Despised

Next door despised
your city. They would much prefer a town.
Your tree – they'd like a twig.
Your oil rig,
your salmon satin crown,
so can you cut it down and cut it down?

Next door began
a harsh campaign. They hired a ticket tout
to sell your oily tree,
your haddocky
crown for a well of drought,
and then they bricked it up and shut it out.

Next door perceived
an envelope was lying on your stoop
but no one wrote to them
so your silk hem
deserved their mushroom soup.
Next door made plans to follow you to group

therapy, pinch
your problems, change their characters and looks.

Next door alleged your streams
gave them bad dreams.
Couldn't you call them brooks?
Couldn't you write some better, shorter books?

Next door observed
your shoulder stump, asked what was up your sleeve,
swore that they meant no harm,
said that to arm
dictators was naïve
(no pun intended). Next door don't believe

you've gone to work,
neither the place nor the activity.
While next door's squirrel slipped,
your manuscript
lolled on the balcony
which might seem natural to you or me

but to next door
it was a gate wide enough to admit
the dwarves in overcoats
who chase weak votes,
whose coffee smells of shit,
whose stubble shakes only when candle-lit.

Next door have got
their own house but they choose to squat in yours.
If you brought up their theft
of what was left
and asked whose ceilings, floors
and walls these were, next door would say next door's.

Like Carnivals

I thought I saw you pass in the parade,
masked on a float or clapping in the crowd,
and was persuaded by the sense it made
that among many, one might be allowed

(one random body at the hotdog stand
or chance extension of the burger queue,
trombone or trumpet player in the band,
even a clown) to turn out to be you.

At all events where people congregate
like carnivals and festivals and balls
I seek our little world within the great,
turning horizons into bedroom walls.

Men to Burn

The same man every year;
though we have men to burn
we have sealed off that idea.
It is still one man's turn.

Every year one man glows,
his bright flesh chars to dim
and every next year shows
we are not rid of him.

He is propped against a fence.
His embroidered teeth still flash.
I part with twenty pence
to convert him into ash

but he won't stay ash for long.
He reappears in rags,
features not quite so strong
and his legs in dustbin bags.

He will keep coming back
for as long as he is allowed.
He will turn from gold to black
if he knows he's got a crowd.

I should have said this before
but I'm not prepared to pay
to bring him back once more
or to make him go away.

I don't like his grey sock face
or this year's cushion knees.
A good man in the first place
makes for better effigies.

Rondeau Redoublé

He likes the soup but doesn't like the spoon.
We hold opposing views on means and ends.
It's funny now, but it would matter soon
If we shared more than chinese food and friends.

In case he breaks the only time he bends,
He drinks the coffee, leaves the macaroon.
He says, as though pure anarchy descends,
He likes the soup but doesn't like the spoon.

I've sat in restaurants all afternoon,
Fallen for all the culinary trends
But to admit this seems inopportune.
We hold opposing views on means and ends.

Normally I am someone who defends
High living, but I let him call the tune
During these strange, occasional weekends.
It's funny now, but it would matter soon;

The earth won't sprout a ladder to the moon
Though we make compromises and amends.
It would be like December next to June
If wé shared more than chinese food and friends.

Sometimes we clash, sometimes our difference blends
And the cold air turns hot in the balloon.
I tell myself (in case success depends
On attitude) that though he hates the spoon,
He likes the soup.

The Norbert Dentressangle Van

I heave my morning like a sack
of signs that don't appear,
say August, August, takes me back . . .
    That it was not this year . . .
say greenness, greenness, that's the link . . .
    That they were different trees
does not occur to those who think
in anniversaries.

I drive my morning like a truck
with a backsliding load,
say bastard, bastard, always stuck
    behind him on the road
(although I saw another man
    in a distinct machine
last time a Dentressangle van
was on the A14).

I draw my evening like a blind,
say darkness, darkness, that's
if not the very then the kind . . .
    That I see only slats . . .
say moonlight, moonlight, shines the same . . .
    That it's a streetlamp's glow

might be enough to take the name
from everything we know.

I sketch my evening like a plan.
I think I recognize
the Norbert Dentressangle van . . .
     That mine are clouded eyes . . .
say whiteness, whiteness, that's the shade . . .
     That paint is tins apart
might mean some progress can be made
in worlds outside the heart.

Steven's Side

I am supporting Steven
as if I were a beam
      under his ceiling, even
though he is not a team.
      Under his ceiling even
a nightmare is a dream.

Steven and I have entered.
Some people have implied
      I would be too self-centred
to cheer for Steven's side,
      I would be too self-centred
to fail if Steven tried.

I am supporting Steven
as if I were a rail
      behind his curtain, even
though he is bound to fail.
      Behind his curtain even
a white net is a veil.

Steven is no performer.
He has no gift for sport.
      I make no cool crowd warmer

by staging my support.
     I make no cool crowd warmer,
adorn no tennis court

but I am supporting Steven
as if I were a pin
     above his hemline, even
though he will never win.
     Above his hemline even
a jacket is a skin.

I am supporting Steven.
I am at Steven's feet.
     I put him first and even
give him a thing to beat.
     I put him first and even
then he will not compete.

Once When the Wind Blew

Our purses and our fumes
distinguish us, the normals, drys and oilies
who scan the tablecloths in auction rooms,
churn up the paper doilies

to find a cleaner head,
phrenology's bald, ornamental scalps,
black virtues sprinkled and black vices spread
on curves as white as Alps.

If we abandoned hair,
if, in its place, we could contrive to grow
lists of our qualities, complete but fair,
best and worst points on show,

the pain that it would save,
the moves from double into separate beds.
Imagine they are coming to engrave,
tomorrow, all our heads

and now's the time to dump
all that we judge unfit for public view.
We're talking ink (an enigmatic bump
is always subject to

interpretation, doubt,
with how it feels depending on the hand).
I would far rather have it all spelled out,
easy to understand.

Would I have felt that twinge
of sadness if I'd seen the word *inert*,
once when the wind blew, underneath your fringe,
or been so badly hurt

if just above your ear
capacity to cause unhappiness . . .
I could extend this game and this idea
but heads do not confess

failings to clumps of hair,
nor leave them stranded when the hair is gone,
but I know yours and when we meet somewhere
I'm going to carve them on.

Over and Elm and I

Nothing to recommend your feet
except that when you put them down
on Market Hill or Benet Street
you make a better town

Nothing to recommend your stance
except that anywhere you stand
soaks up your presence to enhance
all the surrounding land

No evidence you are a cure
but that the envelope you sealed
and hand-delivered to my door
held a St Neots field

Nothing but that you seem to reach
beyond the space you occupy
so that in March and Waterbeach
Over and Elm and Eye

pillows store imprints of your face
surprised to learn that there's a head
whose contact with a pillowcase
can so improve a bed

You hailed a taxi at the lights
now every single cab that turns
on to East Road like yours ignites
Even the downpour burns

In its stone pot the stand-up clock
turns to a flower on its stem
The county's little stations rock
I feel like one of them

The Bridging Line

If, as it now appears,
a second time can lean across the ditch,
retrieve, like a dropped stitch,
the first, long in arrears,
how badly I've misjudged the last five years;

potholes beside our past
I thought they were, when all the time they've been
linear, in between,
travelling (if not fast)
towards next time, back from next time to last.

Tonight's no precipice,
merely one station on the bridging line
where incidents combine,
kiss throws a rope to kiss,
last time connects to next, next time to this –

a better fairytale
than scattered breadcrumbs on the forest floor;
wind howls, rain starts to pour
and soon you've lost your trail.
The bridging line is like a polished rail

beneath our years of space
that I can almost rest my hand upon.
I clutch it now you're gone,
find it reflects your face,
find I believe the next five years will race

straightforwardly ahead
as five have raced straightforwardly behind.
The gaps are redefined.
I hold my breath and tread
the bridging line towards a waiting bed.

The Burning Scheme

The newly burned are queuing in the shop,
leaf-fall-in-autumn jigsaws on their skin.
Everyone only wants the pain to stop
     as they survey the crop
of Delial, Ambre Solaire, Piz Buin.
There is no lotion for the burn within.

The newly dazed are tethered to a wink.
Left eyes stand guard while right eyes squint and seep.
Everything has been tried: pills, a hot drink,
     a cream containing zinc,
everything that is popular and cheap.
The burn within thrives on a good night's sleep.

Moon like an orange in a sea of gin,
apply your coolness to a burning dream.
Hat with a mess thereunder, lift your chin,
     lift all the teeth therein.
How do you fit into the burning scheme,
hat of the famous England cricket team?

The burn within makes no attempt to cheat.
Its pockets, so to speak, are free of sand.

Fairly it wins and squarely it can beat
       every burn caused by heat,
hops on a night flight home, keen to expand
in the wet climate of its native land.

Paint a Closed Window

We stood side by side.
Only George walked on.
You spoke and I replied
            but I had gone.

My gone did not depend
on anything you'd planned
and I did not extend
            even a hand.

My gone was not the sort
that might come back one day.
It was less felt than thought
            but most away.

I looked the same to you,
the arches and the cars,
and you could not see through
            my skin to bars.

My arrow pointed north.
Your word had lost its pass,
so no more back and forth
            from the hourglass.

My face became a chart
where pleasantries were drawn.
The binman pulled his cart
         around the lawn

where we stood once removed,
where we stand twice returned.
Nothing can be improved
         my gone has learned.

Foolish to have supposed
there might be other ways.
Paint a closed window, closed
         is how it stays.

I am prepared to face
how fleeting I have been
to you and to this place,
         that tree, the green

circle of grass, the stone.
From your first fixed-term kiss
I knew I could not own
         any of this.

Minus Fingers

What craftsmen sometimes do to glass
Or children to balloons,
You do (or did, since presents pass –
Shade of infrequent moons),

What lovers, as the distance grows,
Do with a hand and kiss.
Some do to bubbles or a nose
What you have done to this.

What stylists, after wash and cut,
Do to their clients' hair.
What the wind does to make doors shut
Using no more than air.

How brass band players get the sound
Out of their golden horns,
How breezes move one leaf around
Several connecting lawns,

Is how you've treated what you had,
Like football referees
To whistles when a move is bad
Enough for penalties.

You've done what someone does who spends
Money they can't afford.
So let's compare you with said friends
And see how well you've scored.

Your nose is still a chain of blocks.
Your power on the pitch
Is non-existent, Liquid-locks-
For-hair. You weren't once rich

So you enjoyed no spending spree.
You have no crystal zoo.
You can scare no one noisily
Piercing the things you blew.

You've got no notes to make a tune,
No fragile fluid spheres
To demonstrate how fast, how soon
Everything disappears,

No kiss that soars above flat land.
I count what can be shown,
In minus fingers on my hand,
For everything you've blown.

Leaving and Leaving You

When I leave your postcode and your commuting
    station,
When I leave undone the things that we planned to do,
You may feel you have been left by association
But there is leaving and there is leaving you.

When I leave your town and the club that you belong
    to,
When I leave without much warning or much regret,
Remember, there's doing wrong and there's doing
    wrong to
You, which I'll never do and I haven't yet,

And when I have gone, remember that in weighing
Everything up, from love to a cheaper rent,
You were all the reasons I thought of staying
And you were none of the reasons why I went

And although I leave your sight and I leave your setting
And our separation is soon to be a fact,
Though you stand beside what I'm leaving and
    forgetting,
I'm not leaving you, not if motive makes the act.

From *First of the Last Chances*
(2003)

Long for This World

I settle for less than snow,
try to go gracefully as seasons go

which will regain their ground –
ditch, hill and field – when a new year comes round.

Now I know everything:
how winter leaves without resenting spring,

lives in a safe time frame,
gives up so much but knows he can reclaim

all titles that are his,
fall out for months and still be what he is.

I settle for less than snow:
high only once, then no way up from low,

then to be swept from drives.
Ten words I throw into your changing lives

fly like ten snowballs hurled:
I hope to be, and will, long for this world.

Second-hand Advice for a Friend

I used to do workshops in schools quite a lot
And some classes were good, although others were not,
And when sessions went wrong, in no matter what
    way,
There was one standard phrase every teacher would
    say.

Each time couplets were questioned by gum-chewing
    thugs
In reluctant time out from the dealing of drugs,
Some poor teacher would utter the desperate plea:
'Show Sophie Hannah how good you can be.'

This phenomenon cannot be simply explained
Since I don't think it's something they learned when
    they trained.
You do not have to say, for your PGCE,
'Show Sophie Hannah how good you can be.'

You do not have to say it to work or to live
But compared with advice that I've heard teachers give
Such as 'Don't eat in classrooms' or 'Straighten your
    tie',
I've arrived at the view that it ranks pretty high.

Outside the school gates, in the world of grown men,
It's a phrase I'm inclined to recite now and then.
I don't see why I shouldn't extend its remit
On the offchance it might be a nationwide hit.

I've a friend who I reckon could use it. And how.
We've had a nice day so let's not spoil it now.
I am no kind of teacher, and yet I can see
That you're not in the place where you clearly should
    be.

No answering back – just return to the fold.
We'll have none of your cheek and you'll do as you're
    told
By the staff of Leeds Grammar, St Mark's and Garth
    Hill,
All those manifestations of teacherly will

Who join dozens of voices in dozens of schools
That make grown-ups of children and wise men of
    fools.
Stop behaving like someone who's out of his tree.
Show Sophie Hannah how good you can be.

The Shadow Tree

In the lake, a reflected tree dangles
while its counterpart squats on the land.
Together they look, from some angles,
like a hand growing out of a hand.
Trunk to trunk, bark to water, they stand.

One is real, that would be the contention,
while the other, illusion or fake,
is a trick of the light, an invention
of the skin on the top of the lake.
I am here for the shadow tree's sake,

for its unannounced coming and going
(no one plants, no one chops). I would give
anything for a shadow tree, knowing,
as its branches get caught in the sieve
of the surface of water and live

for a glance of the moon, moments only,
that the dark fabrication I saw
was a miracle, not like the lonely
unexceptional lump on the shore,
such a stickler for natural law

with its sap, its botanical listing
and its representation at Kew,
its pedantic disciples, insisting
that one cannot be both false and true.
We are shadow trees. That's what we do.

You Won't Find a Bath in Leeds

From the River Cam and the A14
To the Aire and the tall M1,
We left the place where home had been,
Still wondering what we'd done,
And we went to Yorkshire, undeterred
By the hearts we'd left down south
And we couldn't believe the words we heard
From the lettings agent's mouth.

He showed us a flat near an abbatoir,
Then one where a man had died,
Then one with nowhere to park our car
Then one with no bath inside.
With the undertone of cheering
Of a person who impedes,
He looked straight at us, sneering,
'You won't find a bath in Leeds.'

'We have come to Leeds from Cambridge.
We have heard that Leeds is nice.
A bath is seen in Cambridge
As an integral device,
So don't tell me that a shower
Is sufficient to meet my needs,'

I said. I received a glower
And, 'You won't find a bath in Leeds.'

He fingered a fraying curtain
And I said, 'You can't be sure.
Some things in life are uncertain
And that's what hope is for.
One day I might meet Robert Redford
At Bristol Temple Meads.
I've found baths in Bracknell and Bedford
And I might find a bath in Leeds.'

He replied with a refutation
Which served to increase our pain
But we didn't head for the station
Or run for a rescue train,
Though we felt like trampled flowers
Who'd been set upon by weeds.
We told him to stuff his showers
And we would find a bath in Leeds.

Some people are snide and scathing
And they try to undermine
Your favourite form of bathing
Or the way you write a line.
At night, while you're busy praying
That your every plan succeeds,

There are killjoys somewhere saying,
'You won't find a bath in Leeds.'

A better definition
Might be reading all of Proust,
But the concept of ambition
Has been radically reduced.
While the London wits are burning
Their cash in the Groucho Club,
In Yorkshire we're simply yearning
To locate an enamel tub.

I win, Mr Bath Bad Tiding.
I have not one bath but two.
En-suite in the sweet West Riding
And no bloody thanks to you.
I may never run fast, or tower
Over Wimbledon's top seeds
Or hit sixes like David Gower
But I have found a bath in Leeds.

Wells-Next-the-Sea

I came this little seaside town
And went a pub they call The Crown
Where straight away I happened see
A man who seemed quite partial me.
I proved susceptible his charms
And fell right in his open arms.
From time time, every now and then,
I hope meet up with him again.

Out of This World

Cannot remember grass between my toes
or how it feels when feet and tarmac touch.
Cannot recall my life before I rose
and I have had to rise above so much

that first I hit the roof-rack of the car,
then my ascent bent back a lamp post's head.
I have, without exception and so far,
risen above a tower of what's been said,

above a mountain range of what's been done
to people, books and cities that I love.
I'll risk head-on collision with the sun
if I have one more thing to rise above.

What if the risen suffocate in space?
You send us up, not knowing where we'll go.
Would it be such a terrible disgrace
if just this once, I were to sink below

the quilted warmth of your intended slur,
your next offence, soft as a feather bed?
I'd prove more difficult to disinter
than knobbly tree roots or the tenured dead

and after having done my stint in blue
and subsequent to equal time in green
it will not matter if I dropped or flew
out of this world. Out of this world, I mean.

Everyone in the Changing Room

(11/9/2001)

Everyone in the changing room pronounced it a
       disgrace.
He'll get short shrift in Baildon if he dares to show his
       face.
He needs a damn good seeing to, that's what all his lot
       need,
       Everyone in the changing room agreed.

Everyone in the changing room reckons he's lying low.
The hot ones from the sauna want to tell him where to
       go.
The cold ones from the plunge pool say someone
       should start a fund.
       Everyone in the changing room is stunned.

Everyone in the changing room is certain it was him,
Young mothers from aerobics and the runners from the
       gym
And when they said it's mental, this, and there's no end
       in sight,
       Everyone in the changing room was right.

Everyone in the changing room would fight for this
    good cause.
We swim our lengths and lift our weights; you'll want
    us in your wars.
There will be no more tragedies, no waste or pain or
    loss
        When everyone in the changing room is boss.

Homeopathy

She told me negativity was bad.
I said it wasn't, not the kind I had.

She told me that the people I resent
will have their own accounts of each event.

She said it wasn't up to me to judge
and that I should examine every grudge

and ask myself if those I cannot stand
are those who hold a mirror in each hand

reflecting back to me the awful fact
of who I am, unwelcome and exact.

She said there was no need to feel a threat.
I said suspicion was my safety net.

I'd allow harmless men misunderstood
if she'd allow the opposite of good.

Of course, she said, malevolence exists.
Respond with anger, though, and it persists

whereas apply benevolence like balm
and often you can soothe the rash of harm.

I did not feel my interests would be served
by spreading peace where it was not deserved.

What about standards, justice, right and wrong?
She said our meeting had gone on too long

and that the remedy that she'd prescribed
right from the start, if properly imbibed,

erodes those thoughts that play a harmful role
leaving what's beneficial to the whole

person (in this case, me). If this is true
then since I did just what she told me to –

taking my medicine, the right amount
at the right time – surely she can't discount

the feelings that remain. She should concede
that these must be exactly what I need

and that my grudge, impassive and immense,
is good for me, in a holistic sense.

I proved my point like a triumphant kid.
She laughed a lot. I gave her ninety quid.

The Cancellation

On the day of the cancellation
The librarian phoned at two.
My reading at Swillingcote Youth Club
Had regrettably fallen through.

The members of Swillingcote Youth Club
Had just done their GCSEs
And demanded a rave, not poems,
Before they began their degrees.

Since this happened at such short notice
They would still have to pay my fee.
I parked in the nearest lay-by
And let out a loud yippee.

The librarian put the phone down
And muttered, 'Oh, thank the Lord!'
She was fed up of chaperoning
While the touring poet toured.

The girl from the local bookshop
Who'd been told to provide a stall
But who knew that the youth club members
Would buy no books at all

Expressed with a wild gyration
Her joy at a late reprieve,
And Andy, the youth club leader,
And the youth arts worker, Steve,

Both cheered as one does when granted
The gift of eternal life.
Each felt like God's chosen person
As he skipped back home to his wife.

It occurred to me some time later
That such bliss, such immense content,
Needn't always be left to fortune,
Could in fact be a planned event.

What ballet or play or reading,
What movie creates a buzz
Or boosts the morale of the nation
As a cancellation does?

No play, is the simple answer.
No film that was ever shown.
I submit that the cancellation
Is an art form all of its own.

To give back to a frantic public
Some hours they were sure they'd lose

Might well be my new vocation.
I anticipate great reviews.

From now on, with verve and gusto,
I'll agree to a month-long tour.
Call now if you'd like to book me
For three hundred pounds or more.

Seasonal Dilemma

Another Christmas compromise. Let's drink another
    toast.
Once more we failed to dodge the things that put us out
    the most.
To solve this timeless riddle I would crawl from coast
    to coast:
Which is worse at Christmas, to visit or to host?

To spend a week with relatives and listen to them
    boast,
Try not to look too outraged when they make you eat
    nut roast
Or have them drive their pram wheels over each new
    morning's post?
Which is worse at Christmas, to visit or to host?

Dickens, you let me down. You should have made
    Scrooge ask the ghost
Which is worse at Christmas, to visit or to host?

Dark Mechanic Mills

A car is a machine. It's not organic.
It is a man-made thing that can be fixed,
Maybe by you, as you are a mechanic
Although I must admit that I have mixed
Feelings about your skills in this connection.
You shrug and say my engine sounds 'right rough'.
Shouldn't you, then, proceed with an inspection?
Looking like Magnus Mills is not enough.

Resemblance to a Booker Prize contender
Has a quaint charm but only goes so far.
When servicing formed the entire agenda,
When I had no real trouble with my car,
Our whole relationship was based upon it,
This likeness, but you can't go in a huff
If I suggest you open up the bonnet.
Looking like Magnus Mills is not enough.

I lay all my suggestions on the table:
Fuel pump or filter, alternator, clutch,
The coil or the accelerator cable
Or just plain yearning for the oily touch
Of a soft rag in a mechanic's fingers.
That's not your style at all. You merely grin.

Is it your Booker confidence that lingers?
I don't know why. You didn't even win.

You laugh as if you can't see what the fuss is
When I explain my car keeps cutting out.
I know that Magnus Mills has driven buses;
That's not the way I choose to get about.
I'm sorry that it has to end so badly
But I am up to here with being towed
And I'd take a clone of Jeffrey Archer, gladly,
If he could make my car move down the road.

Ballade of the Rift

Two enemies at once I lost.
It was a heavy price to pay.
I thought that I could bear the cost
Of an impromptu mercy day.
Now I'm invited out to play
And find I feel distinctly miffed
With no fracas, no feud, no fray;
I yearn to instigate a rift.

Wildly and wantonly I tossed
My horde of grievances away.
Above my inner ice and frost
I forged the sun's most radiant ray,
Now, with its heaps of UVA,
Summer's a burden, not a gift.
I miss the grime, the grot, the grey.
I yearn to instigate a rift.

I rue the day I blithely glossed
Over my foes' misdeeds, while they
Try not to boss where once they bossed,
Promise to honour and obey.
To look for peers among one's prey
Requires too great a mental shift,

And as they wheedle, cringe and bray
I yearn to instigate a rift.

Preachers and shrinks and healers say
Forgiveness gives the heart a lift –
Good on them. Be that as it may
I yearn to instigate a rift.

Your Funeral

for L.W.

Since our routine condolences are sent
when someone dies, whether they're young or old,
even if while alive they were as cold
as they are dead, if sympathy's well meant,
why should ungrieving relatives resent
being unnecessarily condoled?

Why should the blood associates get cross
when bland acquaintances at wakes insist
how much the coffin contents will be missed,
how wonderful they were, what a great loss
it is? Form here is all. We can't just toss
bodies away (although we can get pissed

respectfully and in a mournful way).
People are hypocrites. Why should we care?
These days it's not expected that we'll wear
a scrap of black. We're not obliged to say
a single word. We can just look away.
Poor thing, the pain is more than she can bear

some well-intentioned neighbour dressed in black
will squawk, while we, in pinker shades of brown,

watch the undear departed get on down,
thinking of how we wouldn't have her back,
given a god-like choice, not for a stack
of cash, not for a kingdom and a crown.

Confident of the silence I'd maintain,
I was prepared. Then suddenly you die
and even silence seems too big a lie.
My strange regrets chase decades down the drain.
Can you still hear me now if I explain
how much I've always hated you and why?

Of course you can't. There's no such thing as you
or hell, with all its demons and its fears.
I should have told you in the living years,
as Mike and the Mechanics said. How true.
I didn't, though, and so you never knew.
Wreath after wreath arrives and it appears

You got away with it. My mother went
by plane to see you laid to rest abroad.
I told her yet again what I am bored
of telling her, that any money spent
on duty, guilt and other forms of bent
reasoning, one cannot, should not, afford.

She went. She said I didn't understand
and maybe if all mothers were as good
as mine, I would believe all daughters should
behave that well, cross air or sea or land,
even if they're afraid of flying, stand
beside their mothers in their crates of wood,

but when respects can't honestly be paid,
only ensure the death is genuine.
Reserve an empty pocket for a pin
(as did James Coburn in the film *Charade*).
Dig out a shallow oblong with a spade.
Insert deceased. See that deceased stays in.

Now and Then

'Now that I'm fifty-seven,'
My mother used to say,
'Why should I waste a minute?
Why should I waste a day

Doing the things I ought to
Simply because I should?
Now that I'm fifty-seven
I'm done with that for good.'

But now and then I'd catch her
Trapped in some thankless chore
Just as she might have been at
Fifty-three or fifty-four

And I would want to say to her
(And have to bite my tongue)
That if you mean to learn a skill
It's well worth starting young

And so, to make sure I'm in time
For fifty, I've begun
To do exactly as I please
Now that I'm thirty-one.

Wedding Poem

for Rachel and Ian

Marriage's rather grand accommodation
Can make a budding love succeed or fail.
We stumble in and ask for information
Regarding all the properties for sale
And marriage is the price-on-application
Castle with grounds, moat, lake and nature trail.

Some kid themselves and think they can afford it
And when their love runs out it's repossessed
While others, who do better in love's audit
And whose allegiances deserve the best
Because they are the best, those ones can lord it
Over the squabbling and half-hearted rest.

Today the castle has its rightful buyer,
Its asking price, and it will not be trumped
Because the bidding can't go any higher;
This is a love that will not be gazumped
By any other applicant, hard-trier
Or any living heart that ever thumped.

Marriage is love's new house. Love has invested
Its savings wisely, bought the place outright.

It has had several flats, and it has rested
Its head in many a hotel and campsite.
This is the best of all the homes it's tested.
This is where it will sleep now, every night.

Ante-natal

My husband doesn't want to hold the plastic pelvis
      model.
He tells the other husbands that it's bound to be a
      doddle.
He thinks the role of classes is to teach, not
      mollycoddle.
      He'll go so far, but not an inch beyond.

My husband is afraid of meeting women called
      Magenta,
Of sharing wholesome snacks outside the Early
      Learning Centre,
Of any exercise that's an incontinence preventor.
      He's friendly but determined not to bond.

My husband listens to my fear, tells me to overcome it,
Changes the subject to the Davos Economic Summit,
Decides that if there's pain he'll simply ask the nurse to
      numb it.
      He says he doesn't think it sounds that bad.

My husband mocks the books with their advice about
      nutrition,
He shocks the other couples in the coffee intermission

By saying Ziggy Marley seems in pretty good condition
    Despite the smoking habits of his dad.

My husband doesn't care if I'm a leaner or a squatter,
Says pregnancy is no excuse for reading *Harry Potter*.
He isn't keen on Stephanie or Amos or Carlotta.
    Leave it to him; he named our latest car.

On Father's Day my husband gets a card he's not
        expecting.
I say it's from the baby, with a little redirecting.
He doesn't blame my hormones or insist that I'm
        projecting.
    He tells me he's the father of a star.

Mother-to-be

(after reading *New Pregnancy and Birth Book* by
Dr Miriam Stoppard)

Ideally your floors should not be carpeted but tiled.
A brightly coloured nursery will stimulate your child.
Do not eat soft-boiled eggs, smoke crack, fellate
    infected men
But tell your partner how you feel (see diagram, page
    ten).

You're bored and restless? Now is not the time to fly to
    China
Or to let friends with litter trays blow air up your
    vagina.
Make sure your fitness trainer is aware of your
    condition.
Remember, you must check your teeth and call that
    electrician

And every time you raise a glass or lift a fork, please
    think
Is this the very best thing for your child to eat or
    drink?
Once-a-month treats – a slice of cake – will not do any
    harm

But don't lick lambing ewes or stick syringes in your
    arm.

Quite often pregnancies go wrong, and when they do,
    that's sad.
It sometimes happens if you're stressed or pregnant by
    your dad
But eat your folic acid and next time a thin blue line
Appears, relax. Think positive. Most likely you'll be
    fine.

Try not to feel too daunted by this barrage of advice.
It really doesn't matter if you slip up once or twice –
Eat the wrong cheese, go on the game. It's not all doom
    and gloom:
Never again will baby be as safe as in your womb.

God's Eleventh Rule

I want to sit beside the pool all day,
Swim now and then, read *Peeping Tom*, a novel
By Howard Jacobson. You needn't pay
To hire a car to drive me to a hovel
Full of charred native art. Please can I stay
Behind? I will if necessary grovel.
I want to sit beside the pool all day,
Swim now and then, read *Peeping Tom*, a novel.

Pardon? You're worried I will find it boring?
My days will be repetitive and flat?
You think it would be oodles more alluring
To see the chair where Mao Tse Tung once sat.
Novels and pools are all I need for touring,
My *Peeping Tom*, *Nostromo* after that.
Pardon? You're worried I will find it boring.
My days will be repetitive and flat.

Okay, so you were right about *Nostromo*,
But I've a right to stay in this hotel.
Siena: I refused to see *il duomo*.
(Does that mean Mussolini? Who can tell?)
In Spain I told them, 'Baño, bebo, como.'
I shunned the site where Moorish warriors fell.

Okay, so you were right about *Nostromo*
But I've a right to stay in this hotel.

I'm so alarmed, my voice becomes falsetto
When you prescribe a trip round local slums.
Would I drag you from Harvey Nicks to Netto?
No, I would not. Down, down go both my thumbs.
I'm happy in this five-star rich man's ghetto
Where teeth are, by and large, attached to gums.
I'm so alarmed, my voice becomes falsetto
When you prescribe a trip round local slums.

It's not an English thing. No need to grapple
With the strange ways we foreigners behave.
My colleague would be thrilled to see your chapel,
Turrets and frescos and your deepest cave,
But as for me, I'd rather watch sun dapple
The contours of a chlorinated wave.
It's not an English thing. No need to grapple
With the strange ways we foreigners behave.

I want to spend all day beside the pool.
I wish that this were needless repetition,
But next to you, a steroid-guzzling mule,
A hunger strike and the first Christian mission
Look apathetic. God's eleventh rule:
Thou shalt get sore feet at an exhibition.
I want to spend all day beside the pool.
I wish that this were needless repetition.

Equals

Each of my false apologies
I retrospectively withdraw.
Yes, there have been discrepancies
Between my conduct and the law.

I have done worse, I have done less
Than promises would have me do,
And as I cheat, as I transgress
I do not give a thought to you.

I sensed that you deserved it then
But took the blame and looked contrite
Before I did the same again,
Thinking the wrong was mine by right

And I enjoyed the risks I took,
The tricks I played, the daily scam.
I have done nothing by the book.
When I professed to give a damn

My smiles, my tears, my words were fake.
Cut me in half; the core was bad
And when you made your big mistake
I can't deny that I was glad

To see, so newly justified
By your descent from fair and true,
The times I lied and lied and lied,
As if I knew. As if I knew.

Black River

I asked to return to my original love
but I gave the wrong code and access was denied.
The clocks go back, though by no means far enough.
My white form came up green on the other side.
⠀⠀⠀⠀It was so long since I had tried
that to do so was both a relief and a source of pride.

I asked to return to my original niche.
My house and furniture at Black River, I wrote,
then read it through. It read like a limp pastiche.
My white form came out smeared as a ransom note.
⠀⠀⠀⠀I decided I must devote
more time to the box marked *Enter witty anecdote*.

I asked to return to my original ground.
Original, scoffed the clerk, *like there's such a thing*.
I thought his procedures all the more unsound
for being based on a rusty playground swing.
⠀⠀⠀⠀Above us, a blackbird's wing
made a powerful case for never really bothering.

I asked to return to my original point,
but was that a person, a place or a state of mind?
A man in the queue shouted out *Let's split this joint*

so I shared my stash and he left it all behind
       singing *We, the undersigned,*
don't know. Then I wandered off, and what should I
       find?

Well, what I should find (though I cannot say that I did
since the arrows were keen to point towards something
       new
and all known rows, whether Savile, Death or Skid
had become the past, the ephemera and the view)
       is that none of it is true.
Go back to the starting line. Your original love is you.

View

I am not lonely. I pretend
that I am here alone.
I do not see your shuttered face
or hear your monotone

but stare instead at roads and fields
and bridges and the sky
and feel the sun's rays on my face.
However hard you try

to substitute your view for mine,
I see the things I see
and am no longer here with you
though you are here with me.

Metaphysical Villanelle

We may or may not cease to exist.
(conclusion of a long, late-night discussion about
religion on an Arvon course at Lumb Bank)

We have argued for hours and this is the gist.
After much confrontation, at last we agree:
We may or may not cease to exist.

First you scoffed at my view, then in turn I dismissed
Your opinion, but now we've discovered the key.
We have argued for hours and this is the gist:

There is either a god or we're all slightly pissed.
Shall we compromise, since it's now twenty to three?
We may or may not cease to exist.

If I weren't so exhausted I might well insist
That I'm right as a right-thinking person can be
But we've argued for hours and this is the gist:

We can all go to bed without fearing we've missed
Some great spiritual truth. Melvyn's got it, you see –
We may or may not cease to exist.

There isn't a sub-text. There isn't a twist
And who cares? Who would like a Ryvita with Brie?
We have argued for hours and this is the gist:
We may or may not cease to exist.